FINANCIAL PLANNING

FOR YOUR FIRST JOB

MATTHEW BRANDEBURG, CFP®

ISBN: 0615887155
ISBN-13: 978-0615887159

To Renee

FINANCIAL PLANNING
FOR YOUR FIRST JOB

FOREWORD

I thought I was well prepared for entering the "real world" after college. I majored in business and graduated magna cum laude from Bowling Green State University. I thought I knew all the basics when it came to managing my money. I was frugal, a disciplined saver, and lived a modest lifestyle. What else was there to know? Unfortunately, I would find out, a lot.

After graduating from Bowling Green State University I had two job offers. One offer was for a job in procurement at a large pharmaceutical company, and the other was to play professional baseball. I owed it to myself to give baseball a try, despite the horror stories of low pay and long bus rides in the minor leagues. After a handful of successful seasons in the Detroit Tigers minor league system, and one very beneficial trade, I found myself playing in the big leagues for the Florida Marlins just three years after college graduation. Along with my new role as a professional pitcher came a high six-figure salary and a new set of opportunities. I knew it was important that I remain careful with my money so I did not become one of the many professional athletes forced into bankruptcy because they spent their money on cars and bad investments. However, I would soon have my eyes opened to the world of personal finance and learn that financial planning is much more than just saving money.

My first lesson came shortly after being called up by the Florida Marlins. I had never had a credit card in college or the minor leagues, and I thought it was time I start to build credit. I walked into my local bank, sat down with a personal banker, and told him I'd like to apply for a credit card. The first question he asked me was, "What is your annual income?" Thinking my high annual income would warrant a gold or platinum card at the very least, I told him my salary. Unfortunately, after punching a few numbers into his computer, he told me he could not offer me a single credit card. I thought a mistake must have been made. How could I not qualify for a credit card, even one with a miniscule limit? As it turned out, I was ineligible for a credit card because I had no prior credit history.

How could I have not known something like this? Why was I unprepared for something so seemingly very simple? I would find out more about my personal finance assumptions as my first year in the major leagues went on. I found myself with questions about credit, car insurance deductibles, 401k allocations, health insurance, and the onset of a financial recession. I had always paid attention during my college classes, but how to deal with these topics was not discussed. Fortunately, the chapters in this book create a solid foundation for handling your finances and teach you that financial planning is more than just saving money.

Once I learned how many of my assumptions were wrong, I took control of my finances and turned them into a financial plan through the use of this book. Even though baseball careers are short, my financial plan will have me prepared for all aspects of my financial future. I just wish I had read this book before I had to play catch-up.

Burke Badenhop
Pitcher – Milwaukee Brewers

PART 1

SAVING TIME AND MONEY

CHAPTER 1: FINANCIAL PLANNING FOR YOUR FIRST JOB

If you're struggling to make ends meet but can't afford high-priced financial advice, then you've found the right book. Managing your money is easier than you think, and the following chapters will show you how to begin your path to financial independence. Did you know it takes a financial planner an average of three to five years to erase a new client's past financial mistakes? Think about what that means. Not only has the average client made significant financial mistakes in his past, but the mistakes have been so severe that it takes years of work and thousands of dollars to undo them. Think of all the time and money you could save by getting off to the right start today and not having to make up for today's mistakes tomorrow.

TAKING YOUR FINANCIAL SNAPSHOT

In order to manage your financial life you first need to know your starting point. By recognizing where you are today, you'll be able to set tangible goals and track your success from this point forward. To find your starting point, you need to identify your assets, liabilities, income, and expenses. Knowing these items is critical because they help you determine your net worth and manage your cash flow. You can't expect to manage your financial life with any degree of success unless you take the time to complete this all-important first step.

First, focus on your assets and liabilities. Assets are things you own and liabilities are things you owe. Some examples of assets would be your car, laptop, and cell phone. Liabilities would include your car payment, credit card bills, and student loans. Write down all of your assets and liabilities on a sheet of paper and assign dollar values to each of them (see Appendix A: Blank Worksheets). Think of this exercise as taking a *financial snapshot* of your entire life and listing what you see. Once you've written down your assets and liabilities, you can find your net worth by subtracting your liabilities from the value of your assets.

Total Assets – Total Liabilities = Net Worth

Now that you've found your net worth, you have your starting point and can begin tracking your progress from this point forward. Don't be discouraged if you have a very small net worth or none at all today. This book will guide you through the myriad of decisions you'll have to make that will mean the difference between a life of struggle and one of wealth. But if you want to pursue a life of wealth, you first need to decide what that means for you. It's time to define your goals.

DEFINING YOUR GOALS

Take your list of assets and liabilities. Next to them, write down what you would like to own, and the most you feel comfortable owing. The goal of this exercise is to find out what's enough for you. That is, what's enough to get you where you want to be? There's no wrong answer and you don't have to limit your goals to just assets. Think of family, gifts, career, and vacations too. Once you've written down your goals, rank them in order of importance. By writing down your goals and prioritizing them, you're already well on your way to achieving them.

MANAGING YOUR CASH FLOW

You can only achieve your goals if you learn how to manage your cash flow. In fact, cash flow management is the most important part of your financial plan because without it, you'll slip into debt and your plan cannot succeed. By creating a simple cash flow worksheet, you'll be able to quickly identify how much you spend, how much you earn, what your profit or loss is, and how much more you need to earn to turn a loss into a profit.

Tracking your cash flow is easy and only takes a few minutes. You don't need to create a complicated, overly-detailed worksheet. You only need to include enough information so you can see how much you spend and how much you earn. To do this, first write down all of your sources of income and the dollar values attributed to them. Your sources of income include your job, stock dividends, interest, inheritance, scholarships, and gifts. Next, write down your expenses. Don't forget to include all of your expenses such as housing, food, insurance, transportation, gifts, entertainment, and travel costs. Make sure your estimates are correct by referring to old credit card bills, online bank statements, and receipts stuffed away in your desk drawer.

Next, compare your total income to your total expenses to find out what your profit or loss is. If your income is more than your expenses, you have a profit. Otherwise, it's a loss. It's that simple. Once you go through this exercise for the first time, you'll see what your spending habits are and where your *leakage* occurs. Leakage is the few dollars, or *few hundred* dollars, that seems to disappear from your account at month's end, but you're never quite sure where it went.

Don't be discouraged if you have a loss instead of a profit when you complete this exercise for the first time. Now you're armed with the knowledge of what you need to fix, and you can easily determine how much more you need to earn or how much less you need to spend to make your budget work.

TURNING YOUR FINANCIAL DREAMS INTO REALITY

Once you've identified your goals and spending habits, it's time to find out how much work you need to do to turn your financial dreams into reality. This is where the uphill climb begins and your journey can quickly become overwhelming if you don't break down the planning process into manageable steps. An easy way to do this is to compare yourself to a series of financial benchmarks to identify your individual strengths and weaknesses. Comparing yourself to these benchmarks will show you what parts of your financial plan are in good working order and what parts need to be overhauled. Benchmarking allows you to allocate your resources efficiently so you're never sacrificing too much in any single area. See how close you come to meeting the following benchmarks.

- **Cash Reserve**

Have three to six months of living expenses set aside in a savings account or CD as your cash reserve. Consider having three months set aside if there are two income earners in your household and six months if there's only one.

- **Savings**

Save at least 5 to 10 percent of your gross monthly income. This money should be deposited in a savings, investment, or retirement account. (Gross income is your total income before any taxes are paid.)

- **Housing Debt**

Housing debt payments (including mortgage principal, mortgage interest, property taxes, and homeowner's insurance) should not exceed 28 percent of your gross monthly income.

For example, if you earn a gross salary of $50,000 per year, your housing payments should not exceed $14,000 per year or $1,167 per month.

▪ Consumer Debt

Consumer debt payments (including credit cards, vehicle loans, and personal loans) should not exceed 20 percent of your monthly net income. (Net income is the amount that remains after all taxes have been paid.)

For example, if you take home $35,000 per year after tax, your total consumer debt payments should not exceed $7,000 per year or $583 per month.

▪ Total Debt

Total debt payments (housing debt plus consumer debt) should not exceed 36 percent of your gross monthly income.

For example, if you earn a gross salary of $50,000 per year, your total debt payments should not exceed $18,000 per year or $1,500 per month.

▪ Investments

Your total investment portfolio should be at least twenty-five times your annual living expenses by the time you retire.

For example, if you spend $50,000 per year, you should have $1,250,000 in your investment portfolio when you plan to retire.

▪ **Life Insurance**

You should have life insurance equal to six to ten times your gross annual salary to be adequately insured. Keep in mind you may not need life insurance if no one but you is dependent on your income.

For example, if you earn a gross salary of $50,000 per year and your spouse depends on your income, you should have life insurance equal to $300,000 to $500,000 to be adequately insured.

NEXT STEPS

Now that you've given yourself a quick financial checkup, you can see where you need to improve and where you're sacrificing too many of your resources. Compare yourself to these benchmarks every six months or any time you experience a major life event such as marriage, divorce, birth of a child, death of a family member, or job change.

CHAPTER 2: BUILDING YOUR CASH RESERVE

A safety net, or cash reserve, is a must have for your financial plan. During your path to financial independence, you're sure to hit some bumps in the road and that's where your cash reserve comes in. The idea behind a cash reserve is simple. It's making sure you have a "bag of money" big enough to get you through the hard times. And we all have them.

HOW MUCH IS ENOUGH?

To determine how big your cash reserve should be, multiply your monthly living expenses by three to find the minimum cash reserve you should have. If you want to be more cautious, or have only one income earner in your household, set aside six months of living expenses instead. For example, if you spend $5,000 per month, you should have a cash reserve of $15,000 to $30,000.

The cash reserve amount you calculate is your target. It's okay if you don't have that much already set aside. In fact, very few readers will have anything set aside at all when they go through this exercise for the first time. But now you know what your shortfall is and you'll be able to do something about it. Each week, try setting aside just a few dollars.

Within a few months you'll be well on your way to having a comfortable safety net.

You should keep your cash reserve in a savings account or CD at a bank or credit union. These options will allow your money to earn compound interest, which means your money will be working for you even when you're not.

By building a cash reserve, you're providing yourself with options in case unemployment or unexpected bills strike. If you want to know the secret of what financial planners really get paid for, it's this: We provide options to clients. By building a cash reserve, you're providing yourself with a whole new set of options you never knew were missing. You're giving yourself the option to wait for a better job, the option to retire early, and the option to spend more. Most importantly, you're giving yourself the option not to sacrifice your goals when the unexpected occurs.

PART 2

INVESTING

CHAPTER 3: HOW TO THINK LIKE AN INVESTOR

In order to achieve financial independence, you'll need to develop a personal investment plan tailored to your specific needs. The upcoming chapters will guide you through the process of investing and demystify many of the terms you may have heard mentioned among friends or around the office. But before you can develop your personal investment plan, you first need to answer one simple question. Are you a trader or an investor? Consider these factors before you answer: Traders react to short-term changes in the stock market while investors take advantage of long-term trends. Traders buy and sell stocks weekly, daily, or even hourly, while investors use buy-and-hold strategies that lead to investment gains over the long run.

Unless you have extensive knowledge of the stock market and hours a day to devote to research, your safest play is to be an investor. But to be an investor, you first need to know how to think like one. You need to know how to analyze our global economy to see what economic forces are at work. This will allow you to identify the best long-term growth opportunities and create a successful investment plan.

In order to think like an investor you'll first need to choose a trend or economic phenomenon that is of particular interest to you. Take the *green trend* for example. There's been a huge marketing blitz over the past decade encouraging businesses and consumers to "go green" and save the environment. But does this trend have the potential to make you money? To answer this question, you'll need to examine the trend from three perspectives. First, identify the companies you expect will perform well and continue to grow as the trend continues. Second, determine which companies you expect will perform poorly. Third, identify the companies whose futures are uncertain, meaning they could be impacted either positively or negatively as the trend continues. You should avoid these companies until you have more data or the trend stabilizes.

THREE QUESTION ANALYSIS

- **Question 1: Which companies will do well as the green trend continues?**

  1. Companies that are quick to adopt eco-friendly policies
  2. Companies that visibly promote the green trend through mass marketing and advertising
  3. Companies that have the words "green", "solar", or "eco" in their name

- **Question 2: Which companies will do poorly as a result of the green trend?**

  1. Companies that are considered to have high pollution rates—this may include companies in the manufacturing industry

2. Companies that are slow to adopt eco-friendly policies

- **Question 3: Which companies could be impacted either positively or negatively as a result of the green trend?**

1. Companies in the car industry—but why? Because car manufacturers that produce gas-guzzling vehicles will continue to lose business as the green trend gains momentum. However, car manufacturers that focus on alternative fuel technologies and introduce hybrid lines may see increased profits. It's also possible that consumers will rely more heavily on public transportation in the years to come, negatively impacting the auto industry. When you combine these factors, you're left with the impression that it may be too early to tell how the car industry will be affected by the green trend, and uncertainty is an investor's worst enemy.

You should perform a similar three-question analysis for any trend that interests you, in order to determine what types of companies to invest in and what types to avoid. The final step of this process, deciding which individual stocks to buy, requires you to scour the Internet and read newspaper reports until you have a strong indication of each company's financial stability. Read everything you can get your hands on, but make sure it's from a credible source. As a general rule, you should spend at least ten hours researching a potential stock before buying it. (There will be more on buying stocks in Chapter 5.)

This complete process is called *top-down investing,* and it involves looking at the big picture first, then breaking down a trend into smaller details until you finally decide what individual companies to invest in. By becoming a top-down investor, you'll be taking advantage of sustainable market trends and thinking like an investor instead of a trader.

CHAPTER 4: MEASURING RISK

Now that you know how to think like an investor, you're one step closer to developing a successful investment plan. It's now time to examine the second component of investing—risk. When you think about investing, always keep the words "risk" and "return" in mind. The goal of investing is simple. Reduce the risk you're taking while increasing your investment return. But in order to do this, you first need to know exactly how much risk you can tolerate. Answer these five questions to determine your risk tolerance.

- **Question 1: How important is it that your portfolio grows in value over time?**

  Not Important   Very Important
  | 1 | 2 | 3 | 4 | 5 | 6 |

If it's important that your investments are worth significantly more in the future than they are today, choose 5 or 6. If it's not important that your portfolio grows in value, as long as it maintains its present value, choose 1 or 2. If growth is somewhat important, choose 3 or 4.

- **Question 2: How important is low volatility?**

  Very Important   Not Important
  | 1 | 2 | 3 | 4 | 5 | 6 |

How important is it that your portfolio does not experience large swings in value? Within the next few years, if the stock market declined like it did through 2008 and 2009, would you be able to sleep at night? If you can handle these large swings, choose 5 or 6. If you would lose sleep if your portfolio declined in value, even if it later recovered, choose 1 or 2. If you're willing to accept some volatility, choose 3 or 4.

- **Question 3: How important is it that your portfolio generates enough cash for you to live on today?**

Very Important					Not Important
1	2	3	4	5	6

If you're currently using the cash generated by your portfolio to meet your basic living expenses, choose 1 or 2. If you're not, choose 5 or 6. If you might need to use cash generated by your portfolio within the next five years, choose 3 or 4.

- **Question 4: How important is it that your portfolio maintains its current value?**

Very Important					Not Important
1	2	3	4	5	6

If you have $100,000 in your portfolio today, how important is it that at the end of your plan, there's at least $100,000 for you to pass on to heirs or charity? If this is very important, choose 1 or 2. If you would rather spend your last dollar on the last day of your plan, choose 5 or 6. If you fall somewhere in the middle, choose 3 or 4.

- **Question 5: How much risk are you willing to take to achieve a higher return?**

None at All					A lot of Risk
1	2	3	4	5	6

How much risk are you willing to take to get the higher return you want? If you're unable to accept the possibility that your portfolio may lose part of its value on its way to achieving higher returns, choose 1 or 2. If you're willing to take above-average risk for the possibility of higher future returns, choose 5 or 6. If you're somewhere in the middle, choose 3 or 4.

EVALUATING YOUR ANSWERS

Add up your answers and see what your total score is.

Combined Score	Ideal Allocation	% Invested in stocks	% Invested in fixed income	Typical Age
25 to 30	90/10	90	10	35 or younger
15 to 24	70/30	70	30	36 to 55
5 to 14	50/50	50	50	55 or older

This chart shows the maximum percent you should have invested in the stock market according to your risk tolerance. The remaining amount should be allocated to fixed-income investments like cash, CDs, and bonds. The column on the far right shows the age bracket that normally corresponds to the allocation. But keep in mind, each investor is different and your present mood will affect your scores. If you feel your allocation doesn't closely match your attitude toward investing, take the test again in a few days and compare your answers.

CHAPTER 5: BUILDING YOUR FIRST PORTFOLIO

Now that you know how much risk you can tolerate it's time to build the portion of your portfolio dedicated to stocks. Different investments can satisfy this need in your portfolio—stocks, mutual funds, and ETFs (exchange traded funds). Our discussion begins with stocks, and then turns to mutual funds and ETFs.

STOCKS

Buying stocks is a three-step process.
Step 1: Pick the sector
Step 2: Pick the stock
Step 3: Pick the amount

- **Step 1: Pick the Sector**

The first step to buying stocks is identifying the sectors you want to invest in. A sector is a group of businesses in a particular segment of our economy that share similar characteristics. Some examples of sectors include the energy sector (BP and Exxon Mobil), the consumer goods sector (Nike and Polo), and the technology sector (Google and Apple). Other sectors include basic materials, financial services, healthcare, industrial goods, telecom, consumer services, and utilities.

Start by picking sectors you're interested in or that make products you use every day. Find out what companies make these products and write them down. Make sure you pick products from a variety of different sectors to give your portfolio some much-needed diversification.

- **Step 2: Pick the Stock**

Once you've written down the companies you're interested in, you'll need to decide if their stocks are worth your money. You'll have to do research for this step—for many investors this is the fun part. Let's assume one of the stocks on your list is Wal-Mart Stores, Inc. (ticker symbol: WMT). Go to a free stock research website like Morningstar (www. morningstar.com) and find the "Quotes" section. Type in "Wal-Mart" or "WMT" and different charts, graphs, and ratios will appear. You need to locate a few important items.

- *Price*: Can you afford to buy the stock? The price quoted will be how much it costs to buy one share of stock.

- *Industry and Sector*: Remember to pick stocks in different industries and sectors. Wal-Mart, for example, is in the discount store industry and consumer services sector.

- *Five-Year Performance Chart*: The five-year performance chart shows what kind of investment history the stock has had over the past five years. It's important to use the five-year history because the typical market cycle lasts about that long, so you'll be able to see how the stock has performed through good times and bad.

Last, and most important, do your homework. Research the companies you're interested in and find out how they're performing. For Wal-Mart, a search engine like Google will produce over fifty million web hits! Thoroughly research all the companies on your list and identify their strengths, weaknesses, opportunities, and threats (SWOT analysis), so you can decide if their stocks are worth your money.

▪ Step 3: Pick the Amount

Once you've found a group of stocks you want to invest in, you'll need to decide how many shares of each stock you can afford to buy. Remember to be selective and only buy stocks that excel in the areas you researched. As a general rule, you should never have more than 10 percent of your portfolio invested in any single stock. This may be hard to achieve when first starting out, so you may want to test your investing skills with a hypothetical amount of money before entering the "real game".

▪ Don't forget to monitor!

After you've invested your money, you should monitor your portfolio's performance on a weekly basis. There are great account integration websites like Mint (www.mint.com) and Wesabe (www.wesabe.com) that let you to track your entire portfolio for free, and Morningstar (www.morningstar.com) lets you sign up for free email alerts so you can receive an email any time one of your stocks is in the news or releases new financial data. I use these resources every day and wouldn't invest without them.

If you're monitoring your portfolio and see one of your stocks is performing poorly, you have to be willing to pull the trigger and sell. If a stock you're watching loses value over a one year period put it on your watch list. If it goes down for two consecutive years, you may want to consider selling. You may also want to sell if the company gets sued, changes its product, or changes management. These are red flags you can't afford to ignore.

MUTUAL FUNDS

Many investors prefer buying mutual funds instead of individual stocks because of the convenience and instant diversification they provide. A mutual fund is a collection of stocks, and a professional mutual fund manager runs each fund. They are the safe, popular choice for first-time investors, and I highly recommend them. If you're interested in buying a mutual fund but don't already have a specific fund in mind, then you may want to refer to the list of the top twenty-five mutual funds published annually by Kiplinger. The list is available for free at www.kiplinger.com, and it's one of the most valuable mutual fund resources available.

Each mutual fund you research is run by a professional mutual fund manager, and that manager is responsible for deciding what stocks to buy and sell within the fund. You may not have known this, but what stocks each fund manager buys and sells is public information that is available for free to all investors. In fact, a list of each fund's top holdings can be found on almost any stock research website including Morningstar (www.morningstar.com). The top holdings are also listed directly on each fund's website and in their prospectus, which is the fund's primary selling document and acts as the fund's owner's manual. Before you buy a mutual fund, you should research the stocks it owns to make sure they're a good fit for your portfolio.

Once you've found a mutual fund that meets your needs, see if you can afford the minimum investment requirement. If the fund is within your price range and open to new investors, you should go ahead and buy the fund. But if the minimum investment requirement is too high or the fund is closed to new investors, you're not out of luck. Consider buying a few shares of the underlying stocks instead of buying the actual mutual fund. (A word of caution with this approach: Mutual funds can own anywhere from a few stocks to a *few hundred* stocks, so it will be impossible to exactly copy the mutual fund you're researching.)

Studying mutual funds is also a great way to learn from the smartest investors for free. Take Warren Buffett's Berkshire Hathaway fund for example. Just one of his fund's "A shares" will cost you well over $100,000 (ticker symbol: brk.a). But you can see a list of what stocks his fund owns for free, and even purchase a few of those stocks directly for just a few hundred dollars. Of course, you won't have Buffett's expertise of knowing exactly when to buy and sell each stock, but you'll be able to copy his investment style without having to break the bank.

ETFs

Exchange-traded funds (ETFs) are another great way to invest in the stock market, and their ease of use makes them an excellent choice for first-time investors. An ETF is a collection of investments such as stocks, bonds, commodities, or real estate. At first glance, they appear very similar to mutual funds, but ETFs are quickly gaining popularity because they hold a few key advantages over mutual funds, including better tax efficiency, lower expenses, and ultimate flexibility.

- **Tax Efficiency**

ETFs minimize tax implications for investors because they have very low *turnover* compared to mutual funds. Turnover represents how much of a fund's holdings are changed over the course of a year through buying and selling. High turnover should be avoided because each time a holding is bought or sold within a fund there are taxes, commissions, and transaction costs that are passed on to investors. The low turnover and better tax efficiency provided by ETFs make them excellent investments for any type of portfolio.

- **Low Expenses**

The cost of running an ETF or mutual fund is passed on to investors by means of the expense ratio. This number represents the percent of a fund's assets that goes toward paying for the fund to be managed. A typical expense ratio for a mutual fund is about 2 percent, which means an investor's total return will be reduced by 2 percent through the course of the year to pay management fees. Investors should seek funds with low expense ratios so they won't have to sacrifice part of their investment return to pay these high fees. ETFs are a great solution because their expenses are considerably lower than mutual funds. This is because ETFs use indexing strategies instead of individual stock selection so they require less active management.

- **Flexibility**

ETFs are very flexible investments because they allow investors to diversify their portfolios easily by buying into any sector, index, or asset class they prefer. Investors have the ability to purchase ETFs that invest in broad stock market indices like the S&P 1500, as well as those that invest in niche segments of the economy like the telecom and healthcare sectors. If there's a segment of the world's economy you want to invest in, there's an ETF that will let you do it.

- **Beware of Transaction Fees**

Each time you buy or sell an ETF you'll have to pay a transaction fee. The fee varies by investment company, and usually ranges from about $10 to $50 per transaction. The charge is a flat rate regardless of how much you invest, which means ETFs are not good candidates for dollar cost averaging and you should only consider them if you have at least

$1,000 to invest in each fund. Otherwise, the transaction fee may overshadow the low expense ratio ETFs provide. Because there's also a transaction fee when you sell an ETF, you should view these funds as *buy-and-hold investments* and be willing to own them for the long-term.

CHAPTER 6: SHORT-TERM INVESTING

So far, the discussion has been focused on investing in the stock market through stocks, mutual funds, and ETFs. But are these investments suitable if you have a short-term goal? What if you plan to buy a new house next year, should you take a chance by investing your down payment money in the stock market and hoping for the best? Of course not! But finding a suitable alternative can be difficult. This chapter will guide you through the process of short-term investing and show you which investments are appropriate and which you should avoid.

First, we need to define what constitutes a "short-term" goal. In general, if you'll need your money within the next five years you have a short-term goal and should not be investing in the stock market. It's too risky—no matter how great of an investor you are. But where should you invest your money if you'll need it within the next five years? Some possible choices include money market funds, CDs, and bonds. To decide which investment is right for you, consider how many years are left until you'll need your money and then find an investment that matches your required maturity date. For example, if you'll need money for a trip to Europe in two years, buy an investment that lets you select a two-year maturity date, like a bond or CD, to protect your principal. If you find yourself needing a higher rate of return that only the stock market can provide, it means you can't afford what it is you'd like to buy. You don't want to find yourself living beyond your means and relying on the stock market to bail you out—that's gambling not investing. If the stock market underperforms as it has in recent years, you'll find yourself in substantial debt, or having to sacrifice your long-term goals.

LADDERING CASH FLOWS

If you'll need a certain amount of cash each year, for a certain number of years, then follow the strategy known as *laddering your cash flows*. Here's how it works: Consider the case of a recent college grad who plans to go back to school for a four-year master's program. She's received only partial student loans and needs to fund the shortfall from her savings. She estimates that she'll need $5,000 per year, starting one year from today, to pay her tuition bill. She should consider laddering her cash flows by purchasing four CDs that mature one year apart. The first CD would mature one year from today, the second would mature in two years, the third would mature in three years, and the fourth would mature in four years. Each year a different CD will mature and she'll receive enough money to cover her tuition bill for the following year. What she specifically invests in, whether it's a CD, bond, or money market fund, is not as important as the fact she's keeping her money out of the stock market and preserving the principal. Remember, if you'll need your money within the next five years, you should match your investment to your time horizon and avoid the stock market.

❖ ❖ ❖

CHAPTER 7: THE TRUTH ABOUT COMPANY STOCK

If you're considering buying stock in the company where you work, you may want to think twice. Buying too much company stock can be detrimental to your financial plan because it makes you susceptible to certain risks you may not have known about, such as business risk, financial risk, and management risk. Along with these increased risks, there are two reasons why it's best to "just say no" to company stock.

■ **Reason 1: Lack of Portfolio Diversification**

As a young investor, you have limited access to investment dollars; therefore, achieving portfolio diversification should be your primary goal. Portfolio diversification means investing in different stocks, in different segments of the economy, in different economies of the world. As diversification increases, the overall risk of your portfolio decreases. But when you use your limited investment dollars to purchase company stock, you're not achieving diversification unless you're also adding another stock or mutual fund to your portfolio at the same time. This rarely happens because company stock is often purchased automatically through an employer-provided plan, but you may not be enrolled in a similar plan to buy other stocks for your portfolio. Being over-concentrated in just one stock exposes your portfolio to a number of risks that could otherwise be diversified away.

- **Reason 2: Lack of Risk Diversification**

Along with portfolio diversification, you also need risk diversification. This means diversifying the sources of risk that make you susceptible to loss. The principal of risk diversification says that if you're already dependent on your employer for a paycheck, you should avoid becoming dependent on them for the performance of your investments as well. Think what would happen if you were heavily invested in company stock and your company suddenly went out of business. You would not only be out of a job, but your investments would be wiped out as well. Think it can't happen? Just remember Enron, WorldCom, Bear Stearns and Lehman Brothers and how their employees must have felt when their companies suddenly went under.

WHEN BUYING COMPANY STOCK MAKES SENSE

It makes sense to buy company stock if you're able to purchase the stock at a substantial discount from the market price. For example, a 20 percent discount may be enough to offset the increased risks you have to assume when you buy company stock. The second instance is when your company stock fulfills a certain need in your portfolio that can't otherwise be met. For example, if you work for an alternative energy company and your portfolio needs an alternative energy stock for diversification, it may be reasonable to purchase your company stock if you can't find a suitable alternative. But remember, if you choose not to purchase company stock, it doesn't mean you're a bad or disloyal employee, it just means you've done your homework.

CHAPTER 8: HOW TO OPEN AN INVESTMENT ACCOUNT

If you want to invest in stocks, mutual funds, or ETFs, you'll need to open an investment account. Many places allow you to open such an account, and all of them would be happy to have your business. Some of your choices include investment firms, brokerage houses, banks, and insurance companies. Choosing the right company can be difficult, and knowing where to start your search is even harder. The first decision you'll need to make is what *type* of company is right for you. My experience has been that investment firms, banks, and insurance companies charge higher fees and have extra costs compared to brokerage houses. This is because in today's market, investment firms are trying to be banks, banks are trying to be investments firms, and insurance companies are trying to do it all. The result is higher fees and poor service for the average investor.

I recommend opening an investment account at a brokerage house like TD Ameritrade, Charles Schwab, Fidelity, or Vanguard. But even selecting the right brokerage house can be difficult with so many different service platforms available. To make your decision easier, use the questions provided to compare brokerage houses and then select the one that meets your needs the best. It should take less than ten minutes to complete this exercise, and once you're done you'll be able to make a much more informed decision.

What you're looking for is the company that offers the best service, has lowest fees, and provides the easiest access to useful information. Don't be overly influenced by special deals the brokerage houses may be offering today because the deals are usually short-lived, but your account will stay with the company for many years.

BROKERAGE HOUSE COMPARISON

Company name:
Website address:
First impression of website:
Phone number:
Was it easy to reach a phone representative?
Was the phone representative helpful?
Minimum balance required:
Set up fee:
Maintenance fee:
Fee per trade for *no transaction fee (NTF) funds*:
Fee per trade for *transaction fee (TF) funds*:
Extra costs:
Special deals:

- **No Transaction Fee (NTF) Funds**: No transaction fee funds are mutual funds that, by definition, do not require you to pay a transaction fee when you buy or sell them. Whether the transaction is executed by phone or Internet, there should be no transaction fee incurred. You should confirm the brokerage house you choose allows you to buy and sell NTF funds and doesn't substitute their own in-house fee, instead.

- **Transaction Fee (TF) Funds**: Transaction fee funds are mutual funds that require you to pay a flat transaction fee anytime you buy or sell them. Transaction fees range from about $10 to $100 per trade depending on the brokerage house—a reasonable transaction fee is about $15. But keep in mind, there are some very good funds available that don't charge any transaction fee at all. Unless you have at least $1,000 to invest, it's best to avoid transaction fee funds.

CHAPTER 9: YOUR RETIREMENT ROADMAP

The last step to creating your personal investment plan is understanding *why* you're investing. If you're like most readers, you're investing because you know that someday you'll retire and you'll lose your ability to produce income. When that day comes, you need to make sure you have enough savings to carry you through your golden years. Did you know you'll need an estimated twenty-five times your annual living expenses saved up by the time you retire? That's a staggering statistic. For example, if you want to spend $50,000 per year during retirement you'll need at least $1,250,000 saved when you retire! Fortunately, you have time on your side and plenty of years to let your investments grow. But your retirement plan won't come together overnight and it will take years of slow, methodical saving for you to achieve your goal. Even if you can only manage to save $50 per month, you should start chipping away at your deficit today and not put off saving for retirement any longer.

There are two ways you can save money for retirement—through taxable accounts (brokerage accounts, checking, savings, etc.) and through retirement accounts (401k, 403b, IRA, etc.). Taxable accounts are easier for most investors to understand because there is less tax code jargon and IRS rules associated with them. But unfortunately, saving money through taxable accounts alone probably won't be enough for you to reach your retirement goal. This is because part of the investment earnings in taxable accounts are taxed each year, which means less money in your account and less saved when you retire. Retirement accounts, on the other hand, provide tax-deferred growth, so your earnings can grow tax-free each year until you retire and begin making withdrawals. Although there are many different types of retirement plans with hundreds of pages of IRS tax code devoted to them, this chapter will focus on the three most common plans you'll see—the 401k, the traditional IRA, and the Roth IRA.

401K

A 401k is a popular savings plan offered by employers that lets you, the employee, save money for retirement in a tax-advantaged way. Each year you can defer up to a certain amount of your income ($17,500 in 2013) into your 401k, which can then be invested as you choose. The amount of income you defer, along with your investment earnings, avoids taxation until you begin withdrawing money during retirement.

The value of your 401k is based on three factors:
1. The money you contribute through payroll deductions
2. The amount your employer contributes on your behalf
3. Investment earnings on employer and employee contributions

With a 401k, you, the employee, assume the investment risk, which means you must decide how your account should be invested. You'll have a variety of mutual funds, bonds funds, employer stock, and cash investments to choose from based on a list provided by your employer. At the very least, you should contribute enough money to your 401k to take advantage of your employer match. An employer match works just like it sounds. Your employer agrees to match a portion of your contribution and the matched amount gets deposited into your account. This means free money for you, which is something you can't afford to pass up.

If you don't know if your company offers a 401k plan or an employer match, make sure you ask. If such a plan is offered but you're not enrolled, find out how you can enroll today. Under most plans, you must be allowed to enroll by the time you reach age twenty-one or have completed one year of service. Request a copy of the Summary Plan Description (SPD) before you enroll to answer any remaining questions you may have. Remember never to sign up for anything you don't fully understand first.

If your employer doesn't offer a 401k plan, see if they offer a 403b or 457 plan instead. These plans are similar to 401ks but fall under a different section of the tax code and, therefore, have different names. For example, if you work for a university or hospital, you may be offered a 403b plan, or if you're a government employee, you may be offered a 457 plan instead. There are differences between each of these plans, but they all share two important qualities—they let you save money for retirement and defer current income taxes.

ROTH 401K

Beginning in 2006, employers are allowed to offer a Roth 401k instead of a traditional 401k, if they choose. The Roth 401k is a powerful savings tool because it combines the high contribution limit of a 401k ($17,500 in 2013) with the beneficial tax treatment of a Roth IRA, providing the best of both worlds. The downside to participating in a Roth 401k is that any current contributions you make will not be tax deductible. However, you won't have to pay taxes when you withdraw money as long as it's after age 59½, which is the key advantage.

The Roth 401k is valuable if your income is too high to permit a Roth IRA contribution, because the AGI (adjusted gross income) restrictions do not apply to Roth 401ks. A Roth 401k is also beneficial if you're in a low tax bracket today but expect to be in a higher tax bracket when you retire.

Even if your employer doesn't offer a 401k, 403b, or 457 plan, your opportunity to save for retirement is not lost. You can set up your own individual retirement account, known as an IRA, at any brokerage house you choose. There are two main types of IRAs and they are the traditional IRA and the Roth IRA.

✤ ✤ ✤

TRADITIONAL IRA

If you have any earned income this year then you're eligible to contribute to a traditional IRA. It's that simple. The biggest misconception about an IRA is that it's an investment, but instead an IRA is used to buy investments like stocks, bonds, and mutual funds.

▪ IRA Contributions

Each year you're allowed to contribute up to a certain amount of your income to a traditional IRA. For 2013, the maximum contribution is $5,500 or 100 percent of your earned income, whichever is less. The maximum contribution limit is indexed for inflation and changes each year. (Refer to www.irs.gov for current year contribution limits.) Don't be discouraged if you don't have enough money to make a full contribution. Most brokerage houses don't have minimum contribution requirements, so even if you can only afford to contribute $25 per month, you should do it. You have until April 15, 2014 to make your 2013 IRA Contribution.

When you decide to make your IRA contribution, you should call your brokerage house and verify what information you should write on your check in order for your contribution to be processed properly. Each brokerage house is different, but generally, you'll need to write your IRA account number in the memo section of your check along with the words "Year 2013 contribution". Don't staple or attach anything to your check because that can delay processing.

Once your contribution reaches your account, you'll be able to invest the money how you see fit. You can request a list of available investment options from your account provider, but if your IRA is through a brokerage house like TD Ameritrade, Charles Schwab, Vanguard, or Fidelity, you'll be able to choose almost any investment you like with very few exceptions. Some of the exceptions that are not allowed in IRAs include life insurance, precious metals, and collectibles like art and antiques.

▪ IRA Withdrawals

Once your money is invested, it will grow tax-free until you start making withdrawals during retirement. Excluding certain exceptions, you'll have to wait until age 59½ to withdrawal money from your IRA; otherwise, you'll have to pay taxes and penalties. Some of the exceptions that let you avoid the early withdrawal penalty are withdrawals for qualified education costs, excessive unreimbursed medical expenses, or a first-time home purchase.

※ ※ ※

ROTH IRA

Unlike the traditional IRA, not everyone is eligible to make a Roth IRA contribution. You're ineligible to make a Roth IRA contribution if you're single and your AGI is over $127,000. If you're married and file a joint tax return, you and your spouse will be ineligible to contribute to a Roth IRA if your combined AGI is over $188,000. Refer to www.irs.gov for the current year's AGI cutoff.

The Roth IRA is a great savings tool because it lets your investments grow tax-free. While the traditional IRA provides tax-deferred growth, meaning you'll have to eventually pay taxes on the investment earnings when you withdrawal money at retirement, the Roth IRA provides tax-free growth, meaning you'll never have to pay taxes if you follow the rules and make withdrawals after age 59½.

Each year you'll have to decide between contributing to a Roth IRA or traditional IRA. Unfortunately, you can't contribute to both. Generally, you should contribute to a Roth IRA if you qualify because of the tax-free growth it provides. Along with making an IRA contribution, you're also allowed to contribute up to $17,500 to your 401k for 2013. If you max out your IRA and 401k contributions and you're still looking for more ways to save, you can deposit an unlimited amount of money into your taxable accounts (checking, savings, and brokerage accounts) because taxable accounts have no deposit limits.

PART 3

INSURANCE

CHAPTER 10: UNDERSTANDING INSURANCE

When you think about managing your money and creating your financial plan, you need to look beyond just investing and what's in your retirement accounts. Financial planning is a complete process, which means the stock market is just one piece of the puzzle. If your entire financial plan is based only on investing, there's no way you'll survive another recession. It's during difficult times like these that a traffic accident, a house fire, or a medical crisis could devastate your plan if you're not careful. That's why you need to make sure you have adequate insurance coverage that will protect you if an accident or loss occurs. You need to have a few lines of insurance, at a minimum, to protect yourself: auto, homeowner's, health, disability, and possibly life insurance. There are money saving strategies you can employ for each type if you know where to look and what questions to ask.

CHOOSING AN INSURANCE COMPANY

First, you need to know how to choose the right insurance company, or if you've already chosen a company, you need to make sure they're still able to meet your needs the best. There are six factors to consider when evaluating an insurance company and they are:

1. Adequacy of policy limits
2. Cost

3. Potential gaps in coverage
4. Quality of service
5. Company's financial stability
6. Company's claim settlement procedure

Ask your insurance agent to discuss each of these factors as a way to test his ability to effectively communicate with you. If your agent isn't willing to answer your questions now, just think how helpful he'll be when you get in an accident and need to file a claim.

PREMIUMS AND DEDUCTIBLES

Once you've selected an insurance company, you'll need to work with your agent to purchase the combination of policies that are right for you. As part of this process, you'll have to decide what your premiums and deductibles should be. Each year you'll have to pay a *premium* to the insurance company to keep your different policies in force. In return for your premium payment, the insurance company promises to cover you in case of an accident or loss. Premiums work alongside deductibles. A *deductible* is the amount of money you have to pay out-of-pocket when you file a claim before the insurance company will make a payment. A reasonable deductible is $500 for auto and homeowner's insurance. If you have a $500 deductible and file a claim, you'll be responsible for paying the first $500 out-of-pocket and the insurance company will pick up the rest. Deductibles can go as low as $100 or even $0, but choosing a low deductible will make your premium payment much higher. Remember, the lower your deductible the higher your premium.

❖ ❖ ❖

CHAPTER 11: AUTO AND HOMEOWNER'S INSURANCE

AUTO INSURANCE

Auto insurance can be expensive, especially if you're on a tight budget or have recently been in a car accident. Fortunately, you may be eligible for discounts you never knew about. Don't be surprised if your agent never mentioned these discounts to you. You'll have to pick up the phone and ask for them, and you should.

- **Auto insurance discounts are issued for:**

  1. Having air bags, daytime running lights, anti-lock brakes, or an anti-theft device
  2. Being claim free
  3. Having your car and home insured with the same company (the multi-line discount)
  4. Having multiple cars insured with the same company (the multi-car discount)
  5. Having a favorable vehicle injury rating
  6. Driving low miles per year
  7. Being a good student
  8. Being a long-term customer

When you meet with your insurance agent to determine the amount of coverage you need, remember not to choose a deductible that is too low because that will make your premium payment much higher. Ask your insurance agent to provide a quote for what your premium will be if your auto deductibles are $100, $250, $500, and $1,000. There will often be a point where the benefit of having a lower deductible will be overshadowed by the higher premium payment you will owe.

HOMEOWNER'S INSURANCE

Homeowner's insurance is important if someone is injured on your property, something is lost or stolen, or fire occurs. When you meet with your agent to discuss your needs, be sure to review your state property laws to make sure your coverage is adequate and provides for the full replacement cost if your home is destroyed.

Just like with auto insurance, you may be eligible for homeowner's insurance discounts you never knew about.

- **Homeowner's insurance discounts are issued for:**

1. Having a home security system
2. Being claim free
3. Having your home and car insured with the same company (the multi-line discount)
4. Having smoke detectors
5. Living within 1,000 feet of a fire hydrant
6. Living close to a fire department
7. Living in a new home
8. Being a long-term customer

❧ ❧ ❧

CHAPTER 12: HEALTH INSURANCE

You should never go without health insurance. Even if you're young and healthy, it's a risk you can't afford to take. Many different companies offer health insurance, and it can be difficult trying to select one. Contact your local hospital, pharmacy, or clinic and ask what health insurance companies they recommend. Then call these companies and have them explain the different options available to you. You should consider health insurance plans that offer one or two free doctor visits each year along with a free annual checkup. Having prescription drug coverage is also important, but the more features you add on, the more expensive your premium will be.

CHOOSING A HEALTH INSURANCE DEDUCTIBLE

One of the biggest decisions you'll need to make when it comes to your health insurance is deciding what your deductible should be. Remember, the lower your deductible the higher your premium.

A good strategy to select a health insurance deductible is to add up your medical expenses from the past three years and find the average amount you spent per year. This average can be used as your current year deductible if you want to be aggressive and expect to have reduced medical expenses in the upcoming years. If you want to be more cautious, follow the same method, but divide your average expenses in half and make that your deductible instead.

- **Aggressive Strategy:**

    2007: $500 medical expenses
    2008: $1,500 medical expenses
    2009: $1,000 medical expenses
    Average = $1,000
    Deductible = $1,000
    Result: Lower premium

- **Conservative Strategy:**

    2007: $500 medical expenses
    2008: $1,500 medical expenses
    2009: $1,000 medical expenses
    Average = $1,000
    Deductible = $1,000 / 2 = $500
    Result: Higher premium

CHAPTER 13: DISABILITY INSURANCE

The average thirty-year-old has a one in three chance of becoming disabled for more than ninety days before retirement. That's a sobering statistic. It means that between you, your spouse, and your siblings, the odds are overwhelming that at least one of you will face long-term disability before you retire. Being disabled means sacrifice, doctor bills, and having to make difficult personal decisions. How would you answer these questions if you became disabled?

1. Would you continue living in your current house?
2. Could you afford to pay the mortgage?
3. Would you be willing to change your lifestyle?
4. Would your spouse be willing to take a second job?

These are difficult questions, but having disability insurance can make your answers a lot more bearable. Disability insurance will provide you with income each year you're disabled so you can begin living again; it's a necessity for your financial plan. Unfortunately, there's no such thing as a "standard" disability policy and as you shop for coverage you'll find each policy has its own unique provisions. Two of the provisions you need to pay close attention to are the definition of disability and the benefit period. Before you sign on the dotted line, make sure you review these two provisions carefully.

THE DEFINITION OF DISABILITY

Each policy has its own definition of disability, and understanding that definition is critical to separate the good policies from the bad. There are three definitions of disability that you need to know, and they are:

1. Any occupation
2. Own occupation
3. Split definition

- **Definition 1: Any Occupation**

The first definition of disability is known as "any occupation", and it's the least favorable definition for you and the best one for the insurance company. "Any occupation" means that if you become disabled your policy will only pay you benefits if you're unable to perform the duties of *any occupation*. In other words, your skills and training will mean nothing if you become disabled with this kind of policy. For example, consider a surgeon who earns $500,000 per year but gets in a car accident that leaves him severely brain damaged. He's now only capable of mopping the floors in the hospital where he used to operate. Because the surgeon can perform the duties of any occupation (being a janitor), he may not receive disability benefits. For your protection, you should avoid policies that contain the "any occupation" definition of disability.

- **Definition 2: Own Occupation**

The "own occupation" definition of disability is much better for you than the more liberal "any occupation" definition. "Own occupation" means you will receive benefits if you become disabled and you're unable to perform the duties of your own occupation for which you were trained and educated. In the previous example, the surgeon would receive disability income benefits and would not be required to take a lower paying job if he were disabled. For the safety of you and your family, you should consider policies that use the own occupation definition of disability.

- **Definition 3: Split Definition**

The third definition of disability is known as the "split definition" and it's commonly found in employer provided disability policies. A policy with a split definition of disability will pay you benefits if you become disabled and you're unable to perform the duties of your own occupation for a certain period of time (usually two years), and then it will pay benefits if you're unable to perform the duties of any occupation afterwards.

THE BENEFIT PERIOD

Even if you have a policy with the best definition of disability (own occupation), you still may not have adequate protection unless you check the benefit period. Some disability policies will pay benefits for a maximum of five years, while others pay benefits from the time of disability until age sixty-five. Some policies even pay a lifetime benefit, but these policies are becoming less common and more expensive. In general, a five-year benefit period will not be sufficient unless you expect to receive a new source of income afterwards, therefore, you should consider policies with a benefit period to age sixty-five instead.

HOW MUCH COVERAGE SHOULD YOU BUY?

There are limits as to how much disability insurance a company will sell you. The maximum benefit is usually capped at about 60 percent to 66 percent of your pre-disability income. For example, if you earn an annual salary of $50,000 and become disabled, the maximum disability benefit you can receive each year is typically $33,000. This limit may be further reduced if you're a high-income earner, have a dangerous job, or are in poor health. This makes it simple to determine how much disability insurance you should buy—the maximum you can afford.

EMPLOYER PROVIDED DISABILITY COVERAGE

Employer provided disability policies are either *contributory* or *non-contributory*. A contributory policy means that you, the employee, must pay for at least part of the cost of coverage. Unless the definition of disability is "own occupation" and the benefit period is to age sixty-five, you may want to think twice before taking part in a contributory policy.

A non-contributory policy, on the other hand, means you do not have to contribute any money toward the cost of the policy, making it free coverage. Although any future disability benefits you receive will be taxable, it doesn't cost you any money to own a non-contributory policy, so it's usually a good idea to take this coverage. But keep in mind that employer provided disability insurance by itself may not be enough to protect you if it has a poor definition of disability or a short benefit period. You may still need to purchase additional disability coverage through a private insurer.

HOW TO BUY DISABILITY INSURANCE

If you need to buy disability insurance through a private insurer, you should make sure the following questions have been answered before buying coverage:

1. What is the company's quality of service?
2. Is their cost competitive?
3. Is the company financially stable?
4. What is their claim settlement procedure?

Once you find a company you feel comfortable with, you should sit down with an agent and review your options. You need to make sure you find a policy that is tailored to your specific needs. Before you buy a policy, you should read the fine print and double check the definition of disability and the benefit period. Don't forget to ask questions if you don't understand certain details, because once you make your first premium payment it will be too late to change your coverage.

CHAPTER 14: LIFE INSURANCE

Purchasing life insurance without a clear need for coverage is a common mistake a lot of first-time employees make. In general, you only need life insurance if someone else is dependent on your income, you have a specific goal you want to fund at death, or you want to provide enough money to cover your burial costs.

CALCULATING YOUR NEED FOR LIFE INSURANCE

1. Add together your estimated burial costs and any outstanding debts you owe.
2. Multiply the annual amount of income your spouse and dependents will need by the number of years they will need the income. For example, if you want to provide your survivors with $20,000 per year for ten years, you would multiply these numbers together to get $200,000.
3. Add the values from step one and step two.
4. Subtract your current resources, including other life insurance that can quickly be converted to cash to help meet your survivors' income need. (Don't include your car, home, or similar assets if your survivors will need them after you die.) The result represents the amount of life insurance you should consider buying. Review this calculation with your

insurance agent to determine which type of policy is best for you.

The two most common types of life insurance policies are *whole life* and *term insurance*.

WHOLE LIFE VS TERM INSURANCE

If you purchase a whole life insurance policy, it will remain in effect for your whole life as long as you pay the annual premium. When you die, your policy's death benefit will be paid tax-free to your named beneficiary.

Term insurance, on the other hand, means your policy will remain in force for only a specific term of years. Term policies are often issued for periods of five, ten, fifteen, or twenty years. Your beneficiary will only receive the death benefit if you die during the term of your policy. Term insurance is usually less expensive than whole life insurance for individuals in their twenties and thirties.

EMPLOYER PROVIDED LIFE INSURANCE

For employer provided life insurance, a medical exam is usually not required. If you're unable to purchase life insurance on your own, an employer provided policy might be necessary. The most common type of employer provided life insurance is *group term insurance*. "Group" means the amount of insurance provided to each employee must be calculated using a formula that applies to an entire group of employees. This reduces the chance for discrimination.

"Term" means the coverage will last for the term of years you remain employed at your company. If you leave your company, you'll usually have the option to convert your group term policy to an individual policy. The conversion should not require a medical exam, either.

PART 4

MANAGING DEBT

CHAPTER 15: HOW TO MANAGE YOUR DEBT

Debt is a four-letter word we all have to face. Any time we spend more than we make, we're probably making up the difference by going into debt. It's a common problem, but it's something many of us know very little about. If you find yourself in debt, you need to know the right way to pay it off, which involves an easy three-step process you can follow no matter how severe your debt.

- **Step 1: Get Organized**

The first step to managing your debt is to get organized by making a list of everything you owe. Your list should include the lender, outstanding balance, term of the loan, interest rate, and monthly payment for each debt you have. Search through old check registers and online statements to help you remember all your debts such as:

1. Home loans: first mortgage, second mortgage, home equity line, and home equity loan
2. Vehicle loans: car and boat loans
3. Other personal debt: credit card debt, personal loans, student loans, and taxes owed

- **Step 2: Rank Your Debt**

Once you've identified your debts, rank them according to their interest rate from highest to lowest. If you don't know the interest rate on a particular debt, make sure you ask your lender. Knowing your interest rates is the most important part of this exercise because the order you rank your debt becomes the order you should pay them off.

▪ Step 3: Start Paying Off Your Debt

Start paying off your debt based on their rank, with the highest interest rate debt being paid off first. Regardless of the balance you owe, I recommend following this strategy and paying off your highest interest debt first after satisfying all your minimum payments. Others disagree and recommend paying off the debt with the lowest balance first to build momentum. I've never agreed with this strategy and don't like seeing someone pay off a $1,500 student loan growing at 4 percent interest when he has $15,000 of credit card debt growing at 14 percent. The high interest alone could devastate your financial plan if you don't start chipping away at it.

As a general rule, you should pay off your debt more aggressively any time the interest rate you're being charged exceeds the return you're earning on your investments. Assume the average long-term return for the stock market is 8 percent. This means that any debt you have that carries an interest rate higher than 8 percent should be paid off as soon as possible. Even if it means getting a second job or holding a garage sale, you need to do whatever you can to pay off your high-interest debt quickly.

❧ ❧ ❧

CHAPTER 16: UNDERSTANDING STUDENT LOANS

As a first-time employee, you may be planning to go back to school for an advanced degree or you may even have a few years of undergrad still to finish up. The most popular way to fund these education needs is through student loans. But between the fine print and variable interest rates, understanding student loans can be difficult to say the least. If you've started researching student loans, you've probably already discovered the two main types—those that have strict borrowing limits, but offer low interest rates, and those that offer all the money you need (and then some), but charge very high interest rates. So which type is right for you? How can you make sure you select the best loan possible and not make a decision you'll regret later? It will take research and careful planning, but if you follow the outline provided, you'll be able to find the right combination of loans to meet all your needs.

FEDERAL VS PRIVATE LOANS

To start the loan selection process you first need to know about the two main types—federal loans and private loans. Federal loans, also known as Stafford Loans, are provided by the US government and carry a fixed interest rate—currently 6.80 percent. Federal loans allow the borrower to postpone making principal and interest payments until six months after graduation. Private loans are not so generous. They're less regulated than federal loans and often charge high variable interest rates like credit cards, and the interest starts to accrue immediately. You should use private loans sparingly, and only consider them when there's a gap between what federal loans will cover and the final cost of your education.

INTEREST RATE COMPARISON

For student loans, as with most debt, you want to select the loan with the lowest interest rate. The national interest rate for Stafford Loans is currently 6.80 percent, while the average private loan interest rate is 8.00 percent. Stafford Loans have fixed interest rates, while the rates on private loans will change over time depending on the lender and market conditions. The low, fixed interest rates provided by Stafford Loans are an advantage that tips the scale in their favor over private loans. Use a free website like www.bankrate.com to compare the interest rates for student loans in your area.

HOW TO APPLY FOR STUDENT LOANS

When the time comes to apply for a student loan, you should first meet with the financial aid officer at the school you'll be attending to learn about all of your financial aid options. The officer should help you determine if you'll qualify for federal loans based on your current income and the value of your assets. If you won't qualify for federal loans, the officer should provide guidance on what loans you should turn to next, which will probably be a combination of private loans.

If you've narrowed down your list of colleges but haven't made your final decision yet, make sure you meet with the financial aid officer at each potential school to learn about the different financial aid packages available. You'll find that some schools are much more accommodating than others. Once you've done your research, you can apply for a federal loan online by visiting www.staffordloan.com. You'll also be required to fill out the Free Application for Federal Student Aid (FAFSA) form. If you're applying for a private loan, you'll need to communicate directly with the lender, which will usually be a bank or credit union.

UNDERSTANDING THE FINE PRINT

If you've started researching student loans, you may have seen a few words over and over again, but you may not know exactly what they mean. It's important that you understand these words because they can potentially save you thousands of dollars. The must know words are subsidized, unsubsidized, deferment, and forbearance.

- **Subsidized**: Subsidized loans are loans that the borrower does not have to pay interest on while he or she is still in school. Instead, a third party (usually the US government) pays interest while the borrower is in school and interest does not start to accrue until after graduation. You should try to maximize your subsidized federal loans to the fullest extent possible, but beware; these loans are largely based on financial need so you may not qualify.

- **Unsubsidized**: An unsubsidized loan is a loan where the interest starts to accrue immediately, even though payments are not due until six months after graduation. The fact that interest accrues while you're still in school makes these loans less desirable than subsidized loans.

- **Deferment**: A deferment means the borrower can postpone making principal and interest payments on a student loan if certain hardship conditions apply. For example, deferment is allowed if the borrower is still in school, unemployed after graduation, or experiencing economic hardship for up to three years. Even though the borrower isn't required to make monthly payments, interest continues to accrue unless the loan is subsidized.

- **Forbearance**: A borrower may qualify for student loan forbearance if he or she has difficulty making loan payments on time. Forbearance is similar to deferment, but it's granted at the discretion of the lender and documentation is required to prove economic hardship.

COLLEGE FUNDING SUMMARY

If you've decided the pay-as-you-go strategy won't work for your tuition bill and you need the help of student loans, consider using them in the following order.

1. Subsidized federal loans
2. Unsubsidized federal loans
3. Private student loans

Only consider these options after you've met with a financial aid officer and exhausted all possible grants, scholarships, and awards you might be eligible for.

❖ ❖ ❖

CHAPTER 17: PAY OFF STUDENT LOANS OR SAVE FOR RETIREMENT?

One of the most common questions I get from first-time employees is what should they do first, pay off student loans or save for retirement? Today it's common for college grads to owe $50,000, $100,000, or even $200,000 in student loans when they graduate. Unfortunately, given the escalating costs of tuition and the length of time it takes to earn a degree, it's commonplace. If you're like most students, you didn't hesitate to apply for student loans during your first year of college because you thought you'd earn more than enough money after graduation to meet your living expenses, save for retirement, and quickly pay off your loans. But reality isn't always so kind. Now you realize that between taxes and inflation, there's not as much money to go around as you thought. You're faced with a decision. With your limited income, should you pay off your students loans or save for retirement? If this isn't the question you've been asking yourself, it should be.

You know your loans won't repay themselves, but at the same time you need to maintain a lifestyle and try to save some money for retirement. There's just not enough money to go around, therefore, the question becomes one of balance. You need to decide where every dollar of your income will be put to its highest and best use.

You have three options:

1. Pay off your student loans now and save for retirement later.
2. Save for retirement now and pay off your student loans later. That is, make only the minimum student loan payment required.
3. Use a combination of paying off your student loans and saving for retirement at the same time.

Review each of these options to see which is best for you.

- **Option 1: Pay off student loans now and save for retirement later**

Paying off student loans before saving for retirement is a common mistake a lot of college grads make. The reason is simple. When they initially took out their student loans, they convinced themselves the debt would only be temporary and would be paid off within a few years after college. Their goal was to erase the loans and forget they ever happened. But as I said, reality isn't always so kind. Another reason college grads want to pay off student loans before saving for retirement is that they want to get out of debt before they start to save. This is very idealistic, but not very practical. If we all waited until we were debt-free to begin saving, very few of us would ever be able to retire.

But there is a time when it makes sense to pay off student loans first and save for retirement later. This is the right decision if your student loans charge an interest rate that is higher than 8 percent. The long-term investment return for the stock market is about 8 percent, so if you're paying more in interest than you're earning on your investments, your money would be best used paying off your student loans first and saving for retirement later (but not too much later). If you have multiple student loans with multiple interest rates, pay off the loans with the highest interest rates first and put any extra money you have toward saving for retirement.

- **Option 2: Save for retirement now and pay off student loans later**

You should consider this option if the interest rate on your student loans is less than 8 percent. If the average stock market return is 8 percent over the long run, and the interest rate you're being charged is less than 8 percent, then your money would be best used being saved for retirement rather than paying off your student loans. When you factor in the benefits of tax-deferred growth provided by retirement plans, it makes an even stronger case that you should save for retirement first and make only the minimum student loan payment required.

- **Option 3: Pay off student loans and save for retirement at the same time**

If your student loans charge an interest rate that is between 6 percent and 8 percent, you may want to consider a compromise between paying off your student loans and saving for retirement.

Here's an example: Assume you have a $30,000 student loan charging 6.5 percent interest and your minimum monthly payment is $300. You find that after you make the minimum monthly payment and pay your other bills, you still have $100 left over at the end of the month. In this scenario, you should put $50 towards paying off your loan ahead of schedule, and put the other $50 into a retirement account.

CHAPTER 18: BUY OR LEASE?

Buying a new car or a new home can be an expensive and overwhelming experience. It's easy for judgment to become clouded as price negotiations end and financing arrangements begin. It's during this time that first-time employees face one of their most challenging decisions—buy or lease? The buy or lease decision depends on many different factors and it's a decision you can't afford to get wrong. The long-term effects on your credit score, balance sheet, and bank account are too important to take this decision lightly. This chapter will provide the factors you'll need to consider in order to make an intelligent decision and continue on your path to financial independence.

PART 1: BUY OR LEASE A CAR

- **Buying means:**

  1. Higher monthly payments
  2. Limited warranty
  3. Some resale value

- **Leasing means:**

  1. Lower monthly payments
  2. Almost always under warranty
  3. No resale value

- **Factors to consider:**

How long do you plan to drive the car? Short time frames of five years or less favor leasing.

How many miles do you plan to drive each year? Most car leases allow you to drive between 12,000 and 20,000 miles per year. If you exceed the limit, you'll be charged for each additional mile you drive. The penalty for exceeding the mileage limit is typically $0.15 to $0.25 per additional mile, but varies depending on the lease. If you plan to drive your car more than the allotted number of miles, you should consider buying.

Be cautious of lease ads that offer unusually low mileage limits, such as 7,500 to 10,000 miles per year. Although your quoted monthly payment may be lower, you'll be hit with large penalties if you exceed the mileage limit, which cancels out any potential benefit. When deciding between buying or leasing a car, remember the monthly payment alone is not always a good measure.

- **How much car can you afford?**

You should have the sticker price of your new car already saved up in a checking or savings account before you buy or lease. Although you don't necessarily want to pay cash for your new car, you need to have the option available. Otherwise, you'll be buying more car than you can afford and relying on future income and investment earnings to make your monthly payments. This is a quick way to damage your credit score and dig yourself into debt.

Whether you're buying or leasing, consider the amount of money you initially want to put down for your new car. Some dealers require very little at inception or nothing at all, but this may not always be to your advantage. You'll have to factor in the additional interest you'll have to pay over the life of the loan if you make only a small down payment. Use the free down payment calculator at www.bankrate.com/auto to determine your ideal down payment amount.

If you need to finance your new car by taking out a loan, apply through your bank, credit union, or mortgage provider before applying through the car dealership. Compare the interest rates offered by each company and select the one with the lowest rate. You'll find that companies will be willing to offer loans with more favorable terms if you're already doing business with them. Why? Because they can see first-hand what kind of customer you are without having to rely solely on your credit report. They're also afraid of losing your business to their competitors, which increases your bargaining power. Keep in mind your interest rate will depend, to some degree, on the length of your loan. You can expect to pay a lower interest rate for a shorter loan (thirty-six months or less) than you would for a longer loan.

- **Car Buying Tips**

    1. Make a list of the makes and models you're interested in along with the features you want before you visit the car dealership. Be as specific as possible.
    2. Narrow down your search to a few cars, but don't have your heart set on just one.
    3. When you discuss price with the car dealer, ask for a firm quote in writing.

✤ ✤ ✤

PART 2: BUY OR RENT A HOME

- **Buying means:**

    1. Making a down payment and paying closing costs
    2. Monthly mortgage payment
    3. Property taxes
    4. Homeowner's insurance
    5. Maintenance and repair costs
    6. Potential for borrowing through an equity line or equity loan
    7. Tax deductions for mortgage interest and property taxes
    8. The gain on the sale of your home will be excluded up to $250,000 if you're single or $500,000 if you're married.

- **Renting means:**

    1. Making a security deposit
    2. Monthly rent payment
    3. No property taxes
    4. Renter's insurance
    5. Free maintenance and repairs
    6. No potential for borrowing through an equity line or equity loan
    7. No tax deductions for mortgage payments or property taxes because none are paid
    8. No resale value

- **Factors to consider:**

How long do you plan to live in your home? Short time frames of five years or less favor renting.

Can you afford the monthly mortgage payment for a fifteen-year or thirty-year fixed rate mortgage? You should avoid adjustable rate mortgages (ARMs) because the interest rate will change over the life of the mortgage depending on market conditions. The problem with ARMs is that borrowers don't know what their interest rate will adjust to until it's often too late to lock in a better rate. ARMs were partly responsible for the recent housing crisis, because as interest rates adjusted higher, mortgage payments suddenly became too expensive, resulting in delinquent payments and foreclosures. Fixed rate mortgages, on the other hand, are much safer because they allow borrowers to lock in interest rates that never change. If you can't afford the monthly mortgage payment for a fifteen-year or thirty-year fixed rate mortgage, then you may need to rent.

Make sure you understand how expensive home ownership can be. The true cost of home ownership is estimated to be 1 percent to 1.50 percent of your home's value per month. This includes the mortgage payment, taxes, and maintenance costs.

Consider your ability to meet the down payment requirement. You should be prepared to put down at least 20 percent of your home's purchase price as a down payment.

Don't forget to take into consideration non-financial factors, too. Is it important to you that you raise your family in a home you own instead of an apartment you rent? Is there a particular neighborhood you have your heart set on that you can only move into if you buy? Consider similar questions so your family can make the best overall decision. But a few words of caution: Make sure your final decision is not based purely on emotion. It needs to make good financial sense, too.

Whether buying or renting, make sure you address the following questions before committing to a property:

1. What's your commuting distance to work?
2. What's the quality of the general public services in the community?
3. Are there available recreation facilities nearby?
4. What's the quality of the local public school system?
5. What are the latest crime statistics for the community?
6. What's the overall quality of life in the community?

PART 5

SURVIVING A RECESSION

CHAPTER 19: RECESSION-PROOF YOUR FINANCIAL PLAN

In this chapter, the focus turns from financial independence to financial security. When the economy weakens as it has in recent years, it's critical that you have a plan in place to weather the storm. That starts with an understanding that during a recession, you can't take anything for granted, starting with your job. The truth is, during a recession, no one's job is safe. Credit tightens, consumer spending slows, businesses close, and job losses become more widespread. The next time you see this cycle begin, use the following tips to prepare yourself for the possibility of job loss:

- **Increase your cash reserve**

The old adage says you need to have three to six months of living expenses set aside as your cash reserve. Three months if there are two income earners in your household and six months if there's one. But if you feel your job is in jeopardy, that's not enough. You should add at least two months to your cash reserve, which means you should have five to eight months of living expenses set aside at a minimum.

- **Practice living off only one income**

If you have two income earners in your household, practice living only off the income from the job that is the safest.

Consider the second income "a bonus" while it lasts and use it to bolster your cash reserve. This will require changes to your lifestyle and it's best to start making these changes now so you can see what works for you and what doesn't. This will go a long way toward preparing you for the reality of unemployment.

- **Update your resume and cover letter today**

Don't wait until unemployment strikes to start thinking about your resume; you need to start updating it today. You should start your job search the day after you receive your pink slip. It may seem like a rush, but during a recession, it can take weeks or even months to find a new job. This means you need to have your resume and cover letter ready so you can start your search immediately.

- **Find out how much personal health insurance will cost**

When you lose your job, you may be able to continue your employer provided health insurance for a few months under the COBRA rules, but there is usually an extra cost involved. Start checking today to see how much personal health insurance will cost, and remember you should never go without health insurance. You may be surprised to learn how expensive health insurance can be, even if you're young and healthy. Start saving extra when you feel your job is in jeopardy and be prepared to dip into your cash reserve to pay for health insurance if you need to.

- **If you have credit card debt, contact the companies today**

Contact the credit card companies you owe money to and tell them you're facing possible unemployment. Ask them if you can work out a payment plan and find out what the next steps are. Some credit card companies will be willing to work with you if you take the first step, but you must be proactive.

- **Open an individual retirement account (IRA) today**

If you lose your job, you'll lose the ability to contribute to your 401k, 403b, or any other employer-sponsored retirement plan you have. But you don't want to lose your ability to save for retirement altogether. When your cash flow starts to improve again, which it will, you want to have an IRA already set up so you can continue saving.

- **Create a living expense worksheet**

Write down everything you spend money on, starting today. Continue this exercise until you can identify your spending trends. Then look for areas you can improve and ways you can cut back. Having a clear understanding of how much you spend today will help you determine how much you'll need to save if you lose your job.

❖ ❖ ❖

CHAPTER 20: SURVIVING A JOB LOSS

If you lose your job, the first thing you'll need to do is find a way to provide steady cash flow while you get back on your feet. A simple process to accomplish this involves purchasing a series of CDs that mature one month apart. This is called *laddering cash flows* and here's how it works:

First, take the money you have saved up (excluding your retirement accounts) and figure out how many months you could live off it. Then purchase a number of CDs equal to the number of months you calculated minus one. Why minus one? Because you'll need cash to live on from today until your first CD matures in one month. Stagger the maturity dates so that each CD will mature one month after the previous one.

For example, if you have four months of living expenses saved up you would buy three CDs. The first CD would mature one month from today, the second would mature in two months, and the third would mature in three months. Each month, a different CD will mature and you'll receive enough money to cover your living expenses for the following month. Your goal is to get back on your feet before the last CD matures.

As for how many monthly CDs you should purchase, buy as many as you can until your savings are exhausted, up to a maximum of twelve. Once you start doing this, you'll see that laddering CDs provides much needed stability in a time of great uncertainty. There are three reasons this is true. First, it forces you to save and reduces your ability to make impulse purchases. In other words, while your money is invested it's not at your fingertips to spend on something you'll regret later. Second, this strategy provides regular, steady cash flow for you to live on each month. It will feel like you're still receiving a paycheck even though you've lost your job. The only difference is you'll be paying yourself instead. Third, you'll earn a higher interest rate through CDs than you would through a checking or savings account, and you'll be taking advantage of compound interest. Although the interest payments may not seem like much at first, the effects of compound interest will start to put real dollars in your pocket and may even keep you in the black a few extra days.

If you've lost your job and you're starting to ladder CDs, your goal is simple: Land full-time employment before the last one matures. Once you find a permanent job you can stop buying CDs and get back to living your normal life.

CHAPTER 21: RECESSION-PROOF INVESTING

During a recession, the stock market is in freefall and investors wonder how their portfolios will survive. The biggest question on every investor's mind is where they should (or shouldn't) be investing their money. When the US stock market is experiencing sharp losses during a recession, the first place to look for safety is international stocks. Unfortunately, you won't find much help from international stocks during a global recession like the one we faced in 2008. In fact, the losses overseas can be much worse than here in the US. For example, the stock markets of Russia and India fell 72 percent and 65 percent, respectively, in 2008, making investors in the US feel lucky to have *only* lost 40 percent. Seeing these poor returns and reading negative headlines convinces many investors they should sell their stocks and go straight to cash. You don't want to make this mistake.

Disciplined investors know it would be premature to convert to cash without first considering all their investment options. After considering US and international stocks, the next place to look on the investment depth chart are corporate bonds. Struggling corporations that want to stay in business during a recession raise money by selling their bonds to the public. To entice investors to buy their bonds, corporations offer high interest rates. But the high interest rates are accompanied by high risk. For example, during our most recent recession in 2008, investors could have easily purchased five-year corporate bonds that paid well over 10 percent interest per year. That's a tremendous return for a bond, but there's a reason it's so high…it's very risky. What if the company whose bond you purchased goes out of business before the bond matures? You'll lose your money. Think it can't happen? Just ask GM bondholders who thought their investments were as safe as cash, only to find their bonds would be worth just pennies on the dollar a few months later.

If corporate bonds are too risky, investors should next look to government investments like Treasury bills and Treasury bonds. The problem is, during a recession everyone turns to these investments because they're considered the only safe place left to invest. When so many investors turn to Treasury bills and Treasury bonds, the interest rate they pay suffers. In fact, the interest rate fell so much in 2008 that it actually turned negative for short-term Treasury bills. This means that instead of receiving interest, you actually had to pay interest to invest in government securities.

The last place left to turn is cash. But if you sell your investments during a recession and go to cash, you'll be locking in investment losses that you won't be able to recover if there's a rebound. Also, the effects of inflation and taxes will increase your losses even more, only magnifying your problem.

This makes the decision of where to invest during a recession even more difficult, because it seems like there's nowhere to turn. Where to invest during a recession becomes a balancing act, with some US, international, and cash investments needed to add the most value to your portfolio. What portion of these investments you should own depends on your risk tolerance and time horizon. The allocation you choose should soften the blow of future losses and put you in position to take advantage of the stock market rebound when it occurs, which it will. A possible allocation during a recession may be 50 percent in US and international stocks, and 50 percent in cash, CDs, and bonds. This is a much higher cash, CD, and bond position than usual for a young investor, but it may be necessary to survive a recession.

If you're looking for additional ways to recession-proof your portfolio then consider investing in corporate bond funds or using your investment dollars to pay off your debt early. But you shouldn't choose either of these options until you fully understand all the risks involved first.

- **Corporate bond funds:** A single corporate bond by itself may be too risky due to high default risk, but a corporate bond fund can decrease this risk substantially. A corporate bond fund is a collection of hundreds of different corporate bonds. By pooling all these bonds together, the effect of a single company defaulting is significantly reduced. Consider what happens if you own one corporate bond and that company fails. What would happen if that same company fails but it's just one of over five hundred corporate bonds you own?

- **Pay off debt early:** The second option you should consider is paying off your debt early. Even if you have a very low interest rate, you may want to make double payments to retire your debt ahead of schedule because you won't find a positive return in the stock market during a recession. Remember always to compare the interest you're paying against the return you're receiving on your investments. A potential drawback of paying off your debt early is that you may be faced with prepayment penalties, and once your money is out of the stock market it will no longer be available to take advantage of the rebound when it occurs.

HOW LOW CAN THE STOCK MARKET GO?

How low can we go? During a recession, that's the question on every investor's mind. It was certainly the question investors were asking themselves in March of 2009 when the Dow blew through the 7,000 mark and made its way down to almost 6,500. As fear started to set in, investors found themselves wondering where the bottom would be. Was zero an actual possibility?

To answer this question you first need to understand what would have to happen for the stock market actually to go to zero. All stocks would have to become worthless. All of them. In other words, every publicly traded company would have to fail without exception. With all the uncertainty and disbelief in the stock market during a recession, some investors start to think that's a real possibility. But that's not necessarily rational, and a comparison to the Great Depression should explain why.

During the Great Depression, unemployment reached 24.9 percent at its peak in 1933. This meant that a quarter of the workforce was out of work, but more importantly, 75.1 percent of workers still had jobs. In order for the majority of workers to have jobs, companies had to stay in business and earn income to pay salaries, which they did. Compare this to our most recent recession. Unemployment reached 10 percent in 2010, which was the highest level it has been in the past 25 years. But the unemployment rate would have had to more than double to reach the level it was during the Great Depression. And remember, even if that level was reached, businesses would still survive and a majority of workers would still have jobs if the Great Depression has taught us anything. So the next time you get concerned about how low the stock market will go, take a look at the unemployment rate, and see how it compares to the Great Depression. This should ease your fears and give you some much-needed perspective.

WHAT THIS MEANS FOR YOUR PORTFOLIO

If you're an investor wondering where the bottom of the stock market is, you should stop wondering. The truth is, the Dow may go to 6,000, 5,000, 4,000, or even lower, but if you believe business will survive then you also believe the stock market will eventually regain its lost ground. Because you don't know which companies will fail and which will survive, it's important to have a broadly diversified portfolio made up of different stocks, bonds, and cash investments.

Time also becomes a critical factor. If you're investing during a recession and have less than five years until you'll need your money, you'll probably run out of time and won't see a full recovery. But if you're a young investor with over ten years left before you'll need your money, you should recover most, if not all, of your lost gains.

You can significantly reduce your portfolio's recovery time by *dollar cost averaging* into the stock market each month. Dollar cost averaging means buying the same dollar amount of a stock each month, regardless of its share price. This means you'll buy more shares when the stock price is low and fewer shares when the price is high. Dollar cost averaging is a great way to take the guesswork out of investing and avoid market timing.

CHAPTER 22: THE SAVER'S CREDIT

You may be eligible for a valuable tax credit you never knew about called the "saver's credit", which could potentially save you up to $1,000 per year. If you contributed to a retirement plan this year and earned a low or moderate income then you may be eligible to claim this credit. Your eligibility depends on your adjusted gross income (AGI), tax filing status and the other retirement plan contributions you made during the year.

WHO IS ELIGIBLE?

To be eligible for the saver's credit you must be at least eighteen years old and not a full-time student. You also cannot be claimed as a dependent on someone else's tax return. If you meet these criteria, then you're eligible to receive the saver's credit if your AGI is under the following amounts for 2013:

- $29,500 if you are single
- $59,000 if you are married and file a joint tax return
- $44,250 if you are a head of household

WHAT IS "AGI"?

Your adjusted gross income (AGI) is the amount left over after subtracting all eligible tax deductions from your gross income. This means it's possible to earn a high gross income but still qualify for the saver's credit, if you have enough deductions to reduce your AGI below the limit.

HOW THE SAVER'S CREDIT WORKS

The amount of the saver's credit you receive will be 10 percent, 20 percent, or 50 percent of the first $2,000 of retirement plan contributions you made during the year. The highest rate of 50 percent goes to taxpayers with the lowest AGI, and the credit is phased out to 20 percent and then 10 percent as AGI approaches the limits provided.

Single	Joint	Credit Rate
$0 - $17,750	$0 - $35,500	50%
$17,751 to $19,250	$35,501 to $38,500	20%
$19,251 to $29,500	$38,501 to $59,000	10%
Over $29,500	Over $59,000	0%

Once your tax credit is determined, that amount reduces your IRS tax bill dollar for dollar. For example, assume a single taxpayer with an AGI of $16,000 contributed $2,000 to her IRA in 2013. She would be eligible for a 50 percent tax credit on her $2,000 contribution, which is equal to $1,000. This means she can subtract $1,000 from her tax bill to the IRS when she files on April 15. If her AGI was $25,000 instead, she would be eligible for a 10 percent tax credit on her $2,000 contribution, equal to $200.

TOO GOOD TO BE TRUE?

The saver's credit was originally designed to persuade low-income earners to save for retirement. Today, new college grads, employees who were recently laid off, and taxpayers who have many deductions and, therefore, low AGIs, often use the credit.

You should discuss the saver's credit with your accountant, or if you file your own taxes, make sure you know how to claim this credit on the software you're using. In addition to preparing yourself for retirement, you'll be receiving a great tax break that keeps more money in your pocket.

CHAPTER 23: HOW TO HIRE A FINANCIAL PLANNER

If you're losing sleep at night and need help managing your money, you should turn to a certified financial planner. A good financial planner will provide you with peace of mind above all else, but unfortunately anybody can hang a shingle and declare himself a financial planner today. Industry regulations are lax, which means you need to know how to protect yourself and find a planner you can trust. That should go without saying, but in the Bernie Madoff era we live in, it can't be stressed enough. You can search for a certified financial planner in your area by visiting www.cfp.net/search, but even then, you'll need to do careful screening to make sure he or she is affordable and able to meet your needs. Use the following questions provided by NAPFA (National Association of Personal Financial Advisors) to interview potential planners and compare their qualifications and background. Be sure to meet with each candidate face-to-face so you can see their office, meet their staff, and ultimately feel more comfortable with your decision.

INTERVIEW QUESTIONS

1. What is your educational background?
    a. College degree
    b. Graduate degree

2. What are your financial planning credentials, designations, and affiliations?
3. How long have you been a financial planner?
   a. 1 – 4 years
   b. 5 – 9 years
   c. 10 or more years
4. Will you provide references from other professionals?
5. Have you ever been cited by a professional or regulatory body for disciplinary actions?
6. How many clients do you work with?
7. How many meetings will we have per year?
8. What is your method of providing service?
   a. Do you provide a written analysis?
   b. Do you provide recommendations?
   c. Do you assist with the implementation of recommendations?
   d. Do you provide ongoing advice?
9. How is your firm compensated and how is your compensation calculated?
   a. Fee only
   b. Commissions
   c. Fee + commissions
10. Are there any incentives for you to recommend certain financial products?
11. Do you charge a minimum fee?
12. Will you or an associate work with me? (If an associate will be your primary contact, have the associate complete questions 1 – 11.)

❖ ❖ ❖

EPILOGUE: YOUR NEXT STEPS

You now have all the tools you need to put your financial plan in motion. The opening chapter mentioned that it takes a financial planner an average of three to five years to erase a new client's past financial mistakes. Think of all the time and money you could save by getting off to the right start today and not having to make up for today's mistakes tomorrow. Managing your financial plan can easily become an overwhelming experience, but if you break down the planning process into the steps outlined in this book, it will become much more manageable. Remember to stay patient, live within your means, and increase your financial IQ whenever possible.

If the lessons from this book have piqued your interest and you think financial planning may be a career you'd like to pursue, I encourage you to follow your instincts. The number of next-generation planners has steadily grown over the past few years, but more are needed to replace retiring baby boomers. This makes it an excellent time to begin a career in financial planning, and a lucrative one too. Here's an outline of how you can get started in the financial planning profession and what your career path may look like.

BECOMING A FINANCIAL PLANNER

According to *Financial Planning Magazine*, the average income for a financial planner with one to four years experience is $59,000 per year, and those with five to nine years average $112,000. Those who stay in the profession over fifteen years can expect to earn well over $300,000 per year. In fact, financial planning is becoming such a lucrative profession that over 15 percent of financial planners are middle-class millionaires with net worth's ranging from $1 million to $10 million. But breaking into the profession can be challenging. It first requires finding an internship, and usually working without an income for a year or two.

HOW TO FIND AN INTERNSHIP

If you want to become a financial planner, you'll first need to find an internship to gain real, hands on experience. But you won't find the internship you want on any job board or Craigslist. In fact, you should avoid these sources because what you'll find are mostly sales jobs disguised as financial planning opportunities. Instead you'll want to intern at a "fee-only" financial planning firm, which means the company doesn't sell any financial products, but instead provides comprehensive financial planning to clients for a *fee only*. The fee-only business model lets financial planners make unbiased recommendations for their clients and keep their best interests in mind. The challenge with finding an internship at a fee-only firm is that these types of firms usually don't advertise through mainstream media so you may not know they're out there, but they are. Fee-only firms have built their clientele through referrals as opposed to mass marketing, which means you'll have to do a little extra work finding them, but it's worth it.

To find an internship at a fee-only firm, you should locate a list of the top firms in your area as ranked by assets under management (AUM), and then start working your way down the list by contacting each one until you find the internship that's right for you. You can refer to your community newspaper or city magazine for a list of annual rankings. You should also check industry websites like NAPFA (www.napfa.org) and the Financial Planning Association (www.fpanet.org) for a list of firms in your area that may have internships available.

When you find a firm where you'd like to work, introduce yourself as an entrepreneur looking to gain fee-only financial planning experience, and mention you're willing to work for free. Yes, free. In return for providing free labor you'll find a more laid back atmosphere and a time commitment that should be in the range of about ten to twenty hours per week. This is the perfect amount of time because it lets you provide a meaningful benefit to the company while you decide if financial planning is a career you want to pursue full-time. You may even find that a few months of free labor turns in to full-time employment afterward.

▪ Gregg Gonzalez, Senior, Southern Illinois University

I received a phone call from Gregg Gonzalez, a senior at Southern Illinois University, who was searching for a financial planning internship. Gregg was preparing to graduate with a Masters in Economics and Finance, and his short term goal was to find a financial planning internship that would help him turn his educational background in finance into a professional career that helps clients meet their financial goals. Gregg would be a terrific asset to any financial planning firm, but his problem was that job boards were only providing him with leads that turned out to be sales jobs. He decided to follow the strategy provided and went to the NAPFA website to search for fee-only financial planners in his area. By the end of the same day he began his search, he already had two good leads. Gregg wrote, "I sent an email to three of the top financial planners in my area that the NAPFA website listed. I got an email response from one saying there were no positions available at this time, but he [the financial planner] would be more than willing to schedule an appointment to discuss the business and career. I received a phone call from another gentleman saying that, ironically, he had just had an assistant resign and would be willing to schedule an interview next week, which I accepted. He seemed impressed with the fact that I had mentioned the 'fee-only' business model was the type of business I preferred working for."

A week later Gregg was offered the assistant planner position and took the job. Gregg's story is a great example of how easy it is to break into the financial planning profession if you know where to look. If you reach out to the largest and most successful fee-only firms, you'll usually find planners who are more than happy to help you any way they can.

IS YOUR INTERNSHIP A GOOD ONE?

Once you land an internship, you can expect your responsibilities to be limited to scanning and filing client documents at first. But don't be discouraged; these tasks should only last for a month or two. During your next phase, you should find yourself observing client meetings and seeing how planners create financial plans and follow up on client issues. Then, around the six-month mark, you should begin getting to work directly on clients' financial plans under the close supervision of a certified financial planner. This is when the internship starts to become fun and allows for creativity and problem solving. If you find yourself making cold calls and selling only investments or insurance, you should consider finding another internship.

APPENDIX A: BLANK WORKSHEETS

NET WORTH SUMMARY

Assets	Value

Liabilities	Value

Total Assets: $_____   Total Liabilities: $_____

Total Assets $_____ - Total Liabilities $_____
= Net Worth $_____

GOALS

	Short-Term Goals (1-5 Years)	Mid-Term Goals (6-10 Years)	Long-Term Goals (10+ Years)	Rank
Career				
Cash Reserve				
Entertainment				
Family				
Gifts and Charities				
Possessions				
Real Estate				
Retirement				
Vacations				
Vehicles				
Other				

CASH FLOW MANAGEMENT

Income	Amount

Expense	Amount

Total Income: $_____   Total Expenses: $_____

Total Income $_____ - Total Expenses $_____ =
Profit (Loss) $_____

CASH RESERVE

Monthly Expenses x 3 = $_____ (minimum cash reserve)

Monthly Expenses x 6 = $_____ (recommended cash reserve)

Cash Reserve Range:$_____ to $_____

RISK TOLERANCE

1. **How important is it that your portfolio grows in value over time?**

   Not Important   Very Important
      1   2   3   4   5   6

2. **How important is low volatility?**

   Very Important   Not Iimportant
      1   2   3   4   5   6

3. **How important is it that your portfolio generates enough cash for you to live on today?**

   Very Important   Not Important
      1   2   3   4   5   6

4. **How important is it that your portfolio maintains its current value?**

   Very Important   Not Important
      1   2   3   4   5   6

5. **How much risk are you willing to take to achieve a higher return?**

   None at All   A lot of Risk
      1   2   3   4   5   6

   Total Score:

LIFE INSURANCE NEEDS ANALYSIS

1. Final Expenses

Burial Costs $_____ + Debts Owed $_____ = $_____

2. Survivors Annual Income Need

Survivors Income Need $_____ x Yrs to Provide Income _____ = $_____

3. Subtotal

Step 1 Answer $_____ + Step 2 Answer $_____ = $_____

4. Life Insurance Needed

Step 3 Answer $_____ - Current Resources $_____ = $_____

DEBT MANAGEMENT

Lender	Balance	Term of Loan	Interest Rate	Monthly Pmt	Rank

APPENDIX B: 50 WORDS YOU NEED TO KNOW

401k: A retirement plan that allows an employee to put a percentage of earned wages into a tax-deferred investment account provided by the employer. The employee is responsible for choosing the investments.

403b: A retirement plan similar to a 401k plan, but one which is offered by non-profit organizations, such as universities and some charitable organizations, rather than corporations.

Adjusted Gross Income (AGI): A number used to determine your federal income tax. It is your gross income minus deductions.

Asset: Something of value owned by a company (or yourself). Tangible assets include machinery, real estate, inventory, etc. Intangible assets include patents, goodwill, etc.

Asset allocation: The process of dividing investments among different kinds of assets, such as stocks, bonds, real estate, and cash to optimize the risk/reward tradeoff based on an individual's specific investment goals.

Asset class: A type of investment, such as stocks, bonds, real estate, or cash.

Bond: A security that represents debt of the issuer, which can be a corporation, a municipality, or the US government. The issuer is required to pay the bondholder a specified rate of interest for a specified time. When the bond matures, the issuer must pay the bondholder the entire amount of the debt, known as the face value.

Business risk: Risk associated with the unique circumstances of a particular company, as they might affect the price of that company's securities.

Certificate of Deposit (CD): Official receipts issued by a bank stating that a given amount of money has been deposited for a certain length of time at a specified rate of interest.

COBRA: Consolidated Omnibus Reconciliation Act. A health insurance plan that allows an employee who leaves a company to continue to be covered under the company's health plan for a certain time period and under certain conditions.

Consumer debt: Credit card debt + vehicle loans + personal loans = consumer debt

Corporate bond: A bond issued by a corporation. Corporate bonds often pay higher rates than government or municipal bonds, because they tend to be riskier.

Corporate bond fund: A collection of corporate bonds.

Deductible: The amount of money an insured has to pay out-of-pocket when he or she files a claim before the insurance company will make a payment.

Default risk: The possibility that a bond issuer will fail to repay principal and interest to a bondholder in a timely manner.

Deferment: Allows the borrower to postpone making principal and interest payments on a student loan if certain hardship conditions apply. It may be allowed if the borrower is still in school, unemployed after graduation, or experiencing economic hardship for up to three years.

Diversification: A strategy designed to reduce risk by combining a variety of investments that are unlikely to all move in the same direction. Diversification reduces both the upside and downside potential and allows for more consistent performance under a wide range of economic conditions.

Dollar cost averaging: Buying a set dollar amount of a stock or mutual fund on a regular basis. Over time, the average cost will be lower than the average price of the shares because more shares will be bought when the price is low and fewer shares when the price is higher.

Dow Jones (Dow): The most widely used indicator of the overall condition of the stock market. It is a price-weighted average of thirty actively traded blue chip stocks, primarily industrials.

Equity line: A method of borrowing in which a homeowner may borrow against home equity as needed using a checkbook or credit card. It differs from a standard loan in that the borrowing may be done over a period of time, preventing excess borrowing and limiting interest costs.

Equity loan: A loan secured by a primary residence or second home to the extent of the excess of fair market value over the debt incurred in the purchase.

ETF: A mutual fund that tracks an index and is traded on a stock exchange.

Expense ratio: For a mutual fund, operating costs, including management fees, expressed as a percentage of the fund's average net assets for a given time period.

Financial risk: The risk associated with any form of debt financing.

Forbearance: A borrower may qualify for student loan forbearance if he or she has difficulty making loan payments on time. It is similar to deferment, but it's granted at the discretion of the lender and documentation is required to prove economic hardship.

Gross income: An individual's total income before subtracting taxes or deductions.

Housing debt: Mortgage principal + mortgage interest + property taxes + homeowner's insurance = housing debt

Inflation: The rate at which the general level of prices for goods and services is rising, and, subsequently, purchasing power is falling.

Insured: The person, group, or property for which an insurance policy is issued.

Liability: An obligation that legally binds an individual or company to settle a debt.

Management risk: The risks associated with ineffective, destructive, or underperforming management, which negatively impacts shareholders and the company being managed.

Mature: To come due; to reach the time when the face value of a bond or CD must be paid.

Mortgage: A loan to finance the purchase of real estate, usually with specified payment periods and interest rates. The borrower gives the lender a lien on the property as collateral for the loan.

Municipal bond: A bond issued by a state, city, or local government. Municipalities issue bonds to raise capital for their day-to-day activities and for specific projects they might be undertaking.

Mutual fund: An open-ended fund operated by an investment company that raises money from shareholders and invests in a group of assets in accordance with a stated set of objectives.

Net worth: Total assets – total liabilities = net worth

Premium: The amount the insured must pay to keep his or her insurance policy in force. In return for the premium payment, the insurance company promises to cover the insured in case of an accident or loss.

Principal: Face amount of a debt or mortgage on which interest is either owed or earned.

Prospectus: A legal document offering securities or mutual fund shares for sale. It must explain the offer, including the terms, issuer, and objectives.

Recession: A period of economic decline, specifically, a decline in Gross Domestic Product (GDP) for two or more consecutive quarters.

S&P 1500: A stock market index of US stocks made by Standard & Poor's. It includes all stocks in the S&P 500, S&P 400, and S&P 600.

Sector: A group of businesses in a particular segment of the economy that share similar characteristics.

Stafford loans: Federal student loans that are provided by the US government and carry a fixed interest rate.

Stock: A security that represents ownership in a corporation as opposed to a bond, which represents debt.

Subsidized loans: Loans that the borrower does not have to pay interest on while he or she is still in school. Instead, a third party (usually the US government) pays interest while the borrower is in school and interest does not start to accrue until after graduation.

Ticker symbol: The unique letters used to identify a stock or mutual fund.

Treasury bill: A debt obligation issued by the US government and backed by its full faith and credit, having a maturity of one year or less. Treasury bills are exempt from state and local taxes.

Treasury bond: A debt obligation issued by the US government and backed by its full faith and credit, having a maturity of more than seven years. Treasury bonds are exempt from state and local taxes.

Turnover: The amount of a mutual fund's holdings that are changed over the course of a year through buying and selling.

Unsubsidized loans: Loans where the interest starts to accrue immediately, even though payments are not due until six months after the student graduates. The fact that interest accrues while the borrower is still in school makes these loans less desirable than subsidized loans.

ABOUT THE AUTHOR

Matthew Brandeburg is a Certified Financial Planner and President of Bridgeway Financial Group, LLC in Columbus, Ohio. Matthew is the author of the books "Financial Planning For Your First Job", "Your Guide to the CFP® Certification Exam", "CFP® Certification Exam Practice Question Workbook", "CFP® Certification Exam Flashcard Review Books", "Professional Golf Management (PGM) Practice Question Workbook", and "Professional Golf Management (PGM) Interactive Flashcard Book". He is also the creator of the mobile apps "Investment Allocator" and "Pocket Financial Planner". In addition, Matthew teaches the class "Financial Planning in your 20s and 30s" at Ohio State University.

INDEX

CPSIA information can be obtained at www.ICGtesting.com
Printed in the USA
LVOW05s1102090314

376609LV00001B/63/P